Boise State University Western Writers Series   Number 25

John G. Neihardt

By Lucile F. Aly

University of Oregon

Editors: Wayne Chatterton
James H. Maguire
Dale K. Boyer

Business Manager:
James Hadden

Cover Design and Illustration
by Arny Skov, Copyright 1976

Boise State University, Boise, Idaho

Copyright 1976
by the
Boise State University Western Writers Series

ALL RIGHTS RESERVED

Library of Congress Card No. 76 45135

International Standard Book No. 0-88430-024-2

Quotations from *A Cycle of the West* are taken from the 1961 printing by The Macmillan Company; all quotations from Neihardt's work are included by arrangement with the Neihardt Trust.

Printed in the United States of America by
The Caxton Printers, Ltd.
Caldwell, Idaho

2-6-87

John G. Neihardt

John G. Neihardt

In the literature celebrating the rugged spirit and tenacious optimism of the American West, John G. Neihardt, a Nebraska poet, raised one of the most vigorous voices. It sounds in his lyrics and rings through his epic masterwork, *A Cycle of the West,* in blended notes of wonder at the universe and deeper strains of human sorrow. His inspiration came from what he called the "glorious experience of living."

Neihardt's early life prepared him to write about the West and its heroes, for his pioneer heritage gave him a "passionate awareness" of the vast and hopeful West. Born in a two-room house in 1881, he spent his early childhood on his grandfather's farm in Kansas, in conditions not far removed from frontier life. He learned the feel of the prairies as he watched blazing sunsets, heard the "fife-like screech" of wagon wheels on packed snow, knew the sting of the wind, and listened avidly to the tales of old-timers in the warmth of cow-chip fires. Hardships he accepted as "just living"; and he always preferred to remain in the West, where he could shoot game, split his own firewood, and grow his own vegetables.

Neihardt's parents helped to set the direction of his life. On Sunday outings he learned from his father the charm of forest creatures and of rambling over the countryside. One Sunday, when his father took him to a bluff in Kansas City for his first look at the Missouri River, Neihardt's excitement engendered his lifelong interest in the river and in the "richly human saga-stuff" of heroic men who traveled it to explore the West. From

5

his indomitable mother he learned the solid virtue of tempering poverty with resourcefulness and independent spirit. Her gift for creating beauty from almost nothing transformed bare rooms into habitable quarters. Her unceasing struggle to make life mean more than survival instilled in Neihardt both reverence for beauty and respect for honest work. Though not formally educated, she encouraged her son's voluminous reading, and her faith in his gifts sustained him during discouraging moments. From this sturdy heritage he framed his conviction that the world owed nobody a living. His own achievements, he knew, must derive from his own abilities and his own unaided efforts.

Neihardt's sketchy formal education threw him largely upon his own resources. In Wayne, Nebraska, where his family moved after his father's departure, he enrolled in the newly founded normal college before he had attended high schoool. He was younger than his fellow students, but his abilities so markedly distinguished him that the professors guided him into a program of independent studies. For the first time he was exposed to the classics, and his enraptured reading of Virgil set him firmly on the epic path. He was already steeped in Hindu mysticism, due to his early reading of the *Upanishads* and Max Müller's commentary on the Vedanta scriptures. He shared his mother's distaste for "churchy" religion but found the Hindu theories of an integrated universe and a Cosmic Will amenable to his own mysticism. These concepts recur throughout his writings.

Neihardt's ambition to become a poet was kindled in childhood when, in a fever dream, he felt himself flying swiftly through clear air, impelled by a force he was unable to resist. Without fully comprehending the Dionysian implications of the experience, he recognized a creative impulse like the daemon of Socrates prodding him to express an instinctive "truth" he was obligated to impart. He realized, however, that in a small Nebraska town where the arts had small incentive to flourish, an impoverished poet was destined to find himself misunderstood by hard-working neighbors who could not follow him into the world of imagination. He did not question his poetic powers, but he saw that he must prove himself in the world of other men before he could hope to claim their attention. He believed that a poet unable to earn his bread, to roughen his hands by work with the producing earth, had nothing to tell the man in the street. Neihardt was only five feet tall, and his small size troubled him. He adopted a brisk regimen of wrestling, swimming, and walking—twenty miles at a stretch—to make himself strong. He could astound strangers in the tavern with his ten-inch chest expansion, and even outsized bullies learned to respect him.

By 1900, when his family settled in Bancroft, Nebraska, he had already composed his first book of poetry, published with a loan co-signed by his uncle. *The Divine Enchantment,* a "rhapsody" drawn from Hindu sources, recounts the vision of Devanaguy, Mother of Krishna, while she awaits the birth of her child. Not long after its publication, Neihardt became dissatisfied with the book, bought up all the copies he could locate, and burned them. The few survivors are now collectors' items.

Neihardt's first literary reputation came not from poetry but from short stories which he published in such magazines as *The Overland Monthly, The Outing Magazine,* and *The Smart Set.* These were stories chiefly concerned with the fur-trapping period or the life of the Omaha Indians, whom Neihardt had come to know. One of his first jobs, as assistant to a land agent, acquainted him with the Omaha Reservation just outside Bancroft, and the experience aroused his sympathy for the "long hairs," who were clearly being defrauded of their lands. Living for months at a time with the Indians, he listened to their lore, learned their ways, and won their confidence. They named him Little Bull Buffalo, with the acceptance later expressed in the words of an Oglala: "His heart is as Lakota as ours!" In his lyrics, written in early years, Neihardt sometimes adopted the chant rhythms of the Omahas in his experiments with free verse. As his poetic technique matured he moved to traditional prosody, but his prose writings about the Sioux reveal his feeling for the rhythm of their language.

Neihardt's lyrics are informed by lines of thought that characterize his later writings: his mystic's sense of miracle and of the kinship of all nature; his joyous wonder at the glorious privilege of living. His lyrics reveal the loneliness of a young poet yearning for men of larger spirit and wider vision in this grasping world, and they express his stubborn ability to face difficulties without crumbling. His three sequences of love lyrics —*A Bundle of Myrrh* (1907), *Man-Song* (1909), and *The Stranger at the Gate* (1912)—present a fully rounded view of love that ranges from adolescent searching for spiritualized love to finding the ideal in mature love, in marriage, and in the birth of a child. The lyrics open for Neihardt the continuing process ascribed to all sensitive poets by Roy Harvey Pearce of reconciling the exterior material world with the inner world of poetic vision that the poet knows instinctively to be real. Through all Neihardt's writing—epics, drama, and prose—run the major themes of his lyrics: assurance that a master plan guides the universe, belief in the essential nobility of human nature, and faith in the potential of man to rise through reason and insight to what he dreams of being.

The lyrics were written before Neihardt reached the age of thirty, and they belong therefore to his experimental period. As he explored ideas, he tested rhythm patterns, sound and stress combinations, and manipulations of pauses to vary phrase length. Reviews of the lyrics noted flaws of technique but praised their vigor, freshness, and striking imagery. Bliss Carmen, H. L. Mencken, and William Stanley Braithwaite, among others, saw great promise in the young poet. The lyrics do not represent Neihardt's best work, but they are stirring poems, warm with a young man's exuberance and with his yearnings in

8

his quest for values of the spirit. They have received less attention than they merit, possibly because the timing was unfortunate: they appeared before the imagist movement began in America. Neihardt may have been a precursor of the imagists, for many of his lyrics were written in free verse. In the current revival of interest in Neihardt, his lyrics seem to be reaching a new audience.

In 1908 Neihardt married Mona Martinsen, who had known nothing but luxury. The marriage united two people of quite different backgrounds, and its success confirmed Neihardt's faith in perfect love. At eighteen Mona had revealed a talent for sculpture when she molded in bread dough a remarkable likeness of her brother. Her mother then arranged for her to study with a New York sculptor, and later with Rodin in Paris. Upon her return to New York three years later, she read Neihardt's newly published *A Bundle of Myrrh* and impulsively wrote to the poet. He replied, and the paper romance that followed deepened quickly into love. Six months later Mona went to Omaha, where Neihardt met her at the station, license in pocket, and they were married the next day. Life in a cottage without central heat, running water, or electricity did not daunt Mona. She learned to cook and clean, and she took pride in her fine-grained bread and spotless washings. To the end of her life, she considered herself fortunate beyond all other women. The Neihardts enjoyed their four children, and they lived a happy family life even through troubled periods of financial hardship.

In 1912 Neihardt abandoned lyrics and short stories because he believed that a poet at maturity should disavow the subjectivity of lyrics for wider, less personal themes. The cavalry charge of short works, he wrote George Sterling (October 11, 1915), might suffice for dexterous forays to capture the attention of posterity, but such light raids must be backed up by the massive artillery of more expansive works. Casting about for a project to engage his full talents, he wrote two novels, experimented with short plays in verse, and briefly considered a poetic drama based upon the French Revolution. Some of the chants among his last lyrics were composed for possible use in the drama, but since neither the novel nor the drama satisfied him, he decided to follow Mona's advice and his own urgings to write an epic based upon Western history and lore. He had long admired the up-river men of the fur trade, because he thought they were the real explorers of the West—common men, but, in their own right, heroes to equal Homer's.

In 1908 Neihardt had built a boat and traveled down the Missouri River from Fort Benton, Montana, to Sioux City, Iowa, in the voyage recounted in *The River and I* (1908). Following the trappers' river path firmed his conviction that their exploits, and the legends circulated by oral tradition around campfires, were authentic "saga-stuff." Accepting the theory of Jane Harrison and H. M. Chadwick that an "epic period" is a time when a society is cut loose from its roots, Neihardt specified the years of Westward expansion and displacement of the Indians as being the true American epic period. The founding of Eastern colonies seemed to him not to fit the definition, for the colonists carried their culture with them. He described mountain men like Jedediah Smith, Mike Fink, Jim Bridger, and others as "direct descendants in the epic line" of Homer's heroes.

Neihardt understood the hazards of embarking on an epic precisely at the moment when the imagist movement—the "new poetry"—focused literary and critical attention on lyrics, usually in free verse. The epic was generally assumed to be an extinct genre brought to a final if noble end by Milton. The possibility of an "American" epic, though frequently discussed, provoked scant optimism. Neihardt acknowledged that he set himself against the prevailing literary current—took himself "out of the time mood"—by selecting an outmoded genre and writing in rhymed pentameter, a form as thoroughly unpopular as heroic subject matter. But Neihardt had inherited the enterprising

10

spirit of pioneer forebearers who expected to cut their own path through wilderness.

Moreover, he thought it time Americans were reminded of their heritage. George Edward Woodberry's theories of race memory and Carl Jung's discussion of the collective unconscious of the race, as well as current psychic literature on "expanded awareness," convinced Neihardt that Americans had become "hopelessly provincial" in time sense.

He deplored the prevailing fashion among poets and critics, because he believed that it included a dangerous pre-occupation with fragmentary poetry written for an elitist audience of academicians. He had come to disapprove of free verse because he thought it led poets to focus too narrowly upon detail and to disregard form. He considered Whitman the worst possible influence on American literature, for his imitators, without matching his genius, adopted his careless technique.

Another trend, toward intellectual poetry of disillusionment and despair, disturbed him, even in Edwin Arlington Robinson, whose work he admired otherwise. Eliot, Pound, and later the generation of Beat poets, seemed to him misguided and self-pitying. He once described himself as an Unbeat poet. Neihardt defined poetry as song, musical utterance intended to communicate to all readers deep truths of the human heart. For this reason, he called his epic poems songs, and gave attention to the sound of the lines. His belief in a prodding daemon presupposed a wide audience and gave impetus to his sense of mission. The line from a frivolous verse written in his youth —"It's my petted superstition I'm a genius with a mission"— expressed genuine conviction (letter to Bob Davis, January 8, 1906). Years later he wrote: "I have undertaken to preserve a great heroic race-mood which might otherwise be lost. Someone must do this, and I seem to be the one" (see *The Goldenrod*, Wayne State College, December 27, 1920).

In time the daemon became generalized into an assisting

power that Neihardt called "Otherness." He once wrote Frank Luther Mott, "I don't know just what I mean by that 'daemon' business," and added, "anyway, it's glorious to suspect that something stronger than oneself is on the job" (December 14, 1920). His working methods were designed to make him receptive to "Otherness." He confined writing sessions to mornings and isolated himself in a little "office," a one-room structure in the yard of his mothers' house, or in a room apart from family activity.

To recreate the mood, he began each session by reading completed lines in deep concentration, immersing himself in the atmosphere until he reached a near trance state. Then he waited for lines to form in his mind. Polishing each one as it emerged, he perfected it before he moved on. Three lines constituted a satisfactory day's work. Sometimes, if the mood remained strong, he completed ten or twelve lines; but he refused to press his daemon, and he closed his writing for the day when he "felt in his solar plexus" that he must stop. He did not revise. When he wrote the last line of a *Song* the manuscript was ready for type. He believed that in the working state he tapped a higher awareness available to anyone willing to become receptive by submerging himself in a great task.

The writing of the epic *Songs* occupied Neihardt for twenty-eight years, with interruptions dictated by the stern necessity of providing for a family. When he began the epic he was serving as literary editor for the *Minneapolis Journal,* but when he found his entire time pre-empted, he persuaded his editor to let him live in Bancroft and mail in his copy. City life distracted him. He worked most happily in village quiet where he could hear birds sing, could dig in the soil, or could tramp into the woods at will.

After Neihardt had severed connection with the *Journal* in 1920 and had moved his family to the Missouri Ozarks, he financed periods of concentrated writing by making lecture tours.

He commented testily in letters that he was forced to break his train of thought in order to go "shekel-hunting." But the tours allowed him to further his research and to see the country he needed to describe. In Los Angeles he visited A. E. Brininstool, who brought him valuable first-hand material by introducing him to Indians and old campaigners from the Indian wars. In the East his contacts with Major H. S. Lemly, who had witnessed the death of Crazy Horse, brought him acquaintance with other officers who assisted him with details and led him to authentic source materials.

In final form, as published by Macmillan in 1949, *A Cycle of the West* included *The Song of Three Friends* (1919), *The Song of Hugh Glass* (1915), *The Song of Jed Smith* (1941), *The Song of the Indian Wars* (1925), and *The Song of the Messiah* (1935). Neihardt had decided on that final order from the start, but the *Cycle's* chronological order did not correspond with the order of writing. For each *Song*, Neihardt carried on research thorough enough to gain him the respect of historians, who cited him in footnotes and bibliographies. Frederick Jackson Turner sent two students out to talk with Neihardt, after telling them, "The poet is the best historian." Neihardt studied histories and documents of the fur trade, biographies of its central figures, journals of trappers, and records of the Indian Wars. He searched out materials in libraries and traveled over as much of the terrain as he could. He wrote to state geographers and geologists to make certain he did not locate trees, rocks, or shrubs where they could not possibly grow. He checked such details as the color of Indian and cavalry horses, the kind of guns used in battles, and the height and build of individual men.

For his heroes he chose the Ashley-Henry men, the two groups of a hundred each who went up the Missouri from St. Louis in 1822 and 1823 with General Ashley and Major Henry to gather furs along Western streams. Neihardt chose them because they

13

included all the major continental explorers after Lewis and Clark. As a company of stalwart adventurers prepared for hardships and lured by the unknown, they seemed to him "torchbearers of the race" (*The Splendid Wayfaring*, p. 8).

Neihardt gave long thought to a verse form for the epic. He wanted a line long enough to sustain dignity yet flexible enough to guard against monotony. His devotion to Homer and Virgil predisposed him to hexameter, but he recognized that English cadences adapt more readily to pentameter. Consequently, he evolved a form that used the basic techniques of blank verse, but he added two-line rhyme, frequently extended across a section break. He preferred to rhyme the lines because he was convinced that rhyme made for economy and speed, and at the same time added texture to the flow of sound. He called the form rhymed blank verse and disliked intensely hearing it confused with heroic couplet. In his hands the verse did not become monotonous, and as the *Songs* progressed the verse form became increasingly fluent and supple.

In 1913 Neihardt began the first epic, *The Song of Hugh Glass*. He had told the story to Mona, who urged him to "make that man live," and he went to work with an enthusiasm that Frank Luther Mott likened to religious devotion. The real Glass scarcely typified the classical hero. He could not claim noble birth, handsome appearance, nor youth. But he had courage and the capacity for both physical and moral heroism. The *Song* tells the true story of Old Hugh, seasoned trapper and hunter, and his young friend Jamie, a character for whom Neihardt gives no specific historical source. The devotion of the two in the *Song* is fatherly on Hugh's side, hero-worshipping on Jamie's; and their mutual regard takes on poignancy when Neihardt describes Glass as feeling long-buried springs of affection like a barren part of the moon sensing the warmth of a new spring and longing again to be green. Light-hearted Jamie responds like a son.

14

As the trappers move north, Hugh, riding ahead to hunt, is attacked by a grizzly bear and badly mauled. The men find him in a bloody heap, obviously on the point of death. Since the party must move on, two men are detailed to remain and bury Hugh when he dies: Jamie, an immediate volunteer, and the unscrupulous Jules Le Bon, who stays only after a bribe is offered. The two dig the grave, but Hugh Glass lingers. Increasingly restive, Le Bon launches a crafty psychological campaign to persuade Jamie that they must abandon Hugh. He points out signs of weakening in Hugh and of increasing hazard to the burial team, until he completely demoralizes the frightened Jamie. They desert Hugh, Jules confiscating the dying man's rifle, knife, and gear as being of more use to the living than to the dying.

Hugh struggles back to consciousness only to find himself abandoned and bereft of his belongings. Half delirious with rage, dragging a broken leg, he sets out to crawl back to Fort Kiowa—a distance of a hundred miles. His outrage at betrayal so staggers him that the mountains, the desert, and the sky seem to stare with hostility. He toils across barren country, surviving as best he can. As his strength revives, he manages to collect a broken knife and carve a crude set of crutches. Memories of Jamie gradually cease to weaken him and begin to strengthen him, for his "goading purpose" and "creeping pace" teach him to believe in the "miracle of being loved at all" (pp. 185 and 160). When Hugh sees a passing band of Indians as people sharing the hard human condition, he softens. When he cannot kill a straggling squaw for her bits and pieces of survival gear, he reenters the human race, and the scenery no longer glares. At Fort Kiowa he confronts a cowering Le Bon, contemptuously refuses to kill him, and sets out to find Jamie, who has left the fort.

In the Milk River Valley his search ends. Jamie, who had searched frantically for Hugh after he learned of the survival, has been blinded, ironically, by the rifle Le Bon took from Hugh. Jamie lies in a Piegan lodge, sick and broken, waiting for the priest he has begged the Indians to bring. When Hugh enters, Jamie mistakes him for the priest and chokes out the pitiful story of his guilt and of his search for Hugh until the gun blinded him. When he asks whether he has any hope of absolution, Hugh answers that life is too short for harboring hatred. In the concluding moments of the moving scene, Jamie realizes he is not talking to a priest. Hugh reveals his identity and asks, "Will I do?" The blinding of Jamie and the ending are Neihardt's invention. The actual circumstances are unknown, but in the prevailing legend Hugh forgave the youth.

A body of legend has grown up around Hugh Glass, and the story has been retold in numerous versions. The account developed in fullest imaginative detail is *Lord Grizzly,* a novel by Frederick Manfred. In that work, Glass is given a complete past. Neihardt puts more emphasis than Manfred does upon the quality of friendship between Hugh and Jamie, because it is essential to the betrayal theme. Neihardt's *Song* differs from most of the other versions chiefly because its purpose is different. The *Song's* significance does not lie in its plot or characterizations, but rather in its treatment of universal experience and values. Hugh is both himself and mankind betrayed by circumstances and by those he most trusts, denuded of the means to sustain life, and forced to survive by his own exertions. In his struggle Hugh reaches the enduring values that are within the potential of all men.

Although the *Song* fuses poetry and history, its theme is modern, for man's loneliness and sense of betrayal are contemporary themes, and Hugh's struggle to survive is the human condition. On the literal level, his progress across barren country stands as a notable achievement of courage and endurance, but more important, his rejection of hate and vengeance as he learns to value love brings his spiritual growth to the level of magnanimity, the great classical virtue.

The *Song* is also about human achievement, for Hugh learns that accomplishment results not from sporadic effort but from slow movement toward a goal, in the "duty and the beauty of endeavor" (p. 186). What men learn in the journey is more important than the goal attained. Neihardt was talking about himself, too. He was embarking on his own journey in the epic, and the "goading purpose" and "creeping pace" describe his own progress.

At the end of a *Song* Neihardt always felt drained and needed to "fill up" again. In 1916 he discovered the profit in lecturing and made his first western tour. The high plains and rugged mountains impressed him; he was excited by the feel of space. He also discovered that he could be effective on the platform.

By January 1917, he had begun the second epic, *The Song of Three Friends,* which is about the tragedy of Mike Fink, Bill Carpenter, and Frank Talbeau. In one of his early short stories Neihardt had worked out the basic plot and in another had described the dramatic prairie fire of his ending, gleaned from a childhood memory. The events, except for the ending, are documented, and the characters are real. However, the characterizations rest largely on Neihardt's imaginings based on meager source descriptions. In the historical accounts, Carpenter and Talbeau are mentioned only briefly, and the Indian girl, the cause of the tragedy, appears in the single word *squaw*. Fink is the one character developed in the sources: his ruggedly handsome face and physique, his tremendous strength, and his taste for tavern revelry are all detailed. Neihardt elevates his character to a more savory level, though he concedes that Fink is a questionable hero.

The story about Fink and his friends, which opens the *Cycle,* begins with the departure of the first hundred men in 1822.

17

Neihardt draws a lively picture of the St. Louis docks with their keelboats, excited crowds, bustle of loading gear, and farewells as tearful girls cling to their "beardless heroes" (p. 5). The hundred singing men begin their journey, and among them go the three friends—Fink, the embodiment of "God's Adamic dream" (p. 13); Carpenter, a six-foot "cedar of a man" (p. 11), who is without Fink's ability with words or ready wit, but who is gravely competent; and Talbeau, a wiry little man with Neihardt's ability to hold his own against bulky opponents by speed of movement. So firm is their friendship that Fink and Carpenter frequently close their wrangles with a ritual of facing each other at sixty paces, one friend shooting a cup of whiskey off the other's head.

The three friends undertake a special mission to a Blood village, where the tragedy is set in motion. Mike, the carouser with "blowsy Ariadnes," sees the beautiful foster daughter of a chief and looks on "rum that was not rum" (pp. 40 and 43). Genuine love touches him, and his world turns "wonderful and strange" (p. 40). Unfortunately, the girl fixes her heart on Carpenter, and Fink's anger destroys the friendship.

Talbeau seeks in vain to restore amicability. Mike's rage is caused by wounded pride, not jealousy, and the girl's rejection of his serious love marks the first time his superior manhood has been called into question. His frustration erupts into violence, and he loses to Carpenter in a bloody fistfight. When spring seems to revive good spirits, Talbeau, misled by Fink's apparent relenting, suggests shooting the cup in order to cement this restored friendship. A flip of the coin gives Fink the chance to shoot. Perhaps with some premonition, Carpenter wills his gun and gear to Talbeau if Mike misses; then Mike fires, and Carpenter falls dead. Neihardt follows the sources in showing Mike as throwing down his gun, cursing, and protesting that he did not mean to kill, but the poet departs from the record in the remaining events.

18

In the source accounts, Mike, during a drunken spree, boasted of killing Carpenter on purpose, and Talbeau at once shot him. In the *Song* the vengeance is delayed for dramatic effect. Mike and Talbeau are sent to meet Ashley. On the journey Talbeau is troubled by dreams of Carpenter; and once, both men dream that Carpenter, with a cup on his head, is smiling at them. When they wake to find a prairie fire raging toward them, Talbeau thinks that Carpenter has tried to warn them.

They flee the fire and save themselves by scrambling up a butte. When they descend to ruined country, recover their gear, and stop to rest, Talbeau's persistent talk of Carpenter irritates Fink until he blurts out that he had killed Carpenter intentionally. Distraught, Talbeau becomes obsessed with the belief that he has been given the task of avenging the murder. With the point of his rifle he orders Fink out into the charred countryside. Whenever Fink pauses in flight Talbeau prods him on with well placed shots. The terrified Fink runs through the nightmare country, goaded by the feeling that eyes are watching him. Gradually the eyes become his own accusing guilt, and he flees his deed, more fearful of night and dreams of eyes upon him than fearful of Talbeau.

Eventually Talbeau begins to pity Fink and to repent his vengeance. When he sees that he has no right to play God, he pursues Fink to make amends. But he has repented too late. In horror he discovers the remains of Mike, and the *Song* closes on his wail of anguish, answered by jeering crows.

Of all the *Songs, The Song of Three Friends* follows most closely the classical epic tradition. The frank brutality of the action and the dominant masculinity of the story make its tone Greek. Neihardt wrote it in the early years of his friendship with Julius T. House, an enthusiastic Greek scholar; and House's influence may partly explain the conscious echoes of Greek epics. The pictures of trappers around the campfire spinning yarns or engaging in sports and merrymaking recall Homeric passages, and the frequent comments to the reader that predict either impending doom or the interference of chance parallel choric notes in classical epics. Still, the tragedy is modern in that it locates the causes of men's behavior in the human mind and heart; for the three friends, authentic heroes in physical courage, come to grief because they lack the moral force to solve problems too great for their understanding.

Neihardt believed in a vertical, not a horizontal, scale of values. In the *Cycle* he intended a progression in spiritual insight along with the time-space progression. In this *Song* he treated the lowest level of values in extolling physical courage, for courage, however indispensable, cannot prevent disaster that must be averted by higher levels of virtue. Fink, falling prey to wounded pride, Carpenter, victimized by a fatal inarticulateness, and Talbeau, misled by vengeful obsession, create the tragedy. At the end, Talbeau's comprehension that he has usurped power not his to command foreshadows the rise in the level of values achieved in Hugh Glass's magnanimity.

Neihardt's completion of the second *Song* roughly coincided with his move to Branson, Missouri, in the Ozarks, where he could work in greater seclusion and could enjoy a milder climate than Nebraska offered. He built a studio for Mona's work, and he collected a family of animals including a Jersey cow, a goat, horses, and assorted small pets. In the five years which he devoted to writing *The Song of the Indian Wars,* he worked with fewer interruptions than ever before, or after. He derived some income from book reviews, but he financed the writing periods chiefly by lecture tours. When he had piled up enough money, he made undisturbed progress until funds thinned out; then he scheduled another tour.

The intervals of steady work allowed him to write with joyous abandonment, his exhilaration spilling out in letters. "It's great to have a big job to do," he wrote, "and to know how to do it." Predicting that the *Song* would be a "he-moose," he exulted, "Lord! what material—what wonderful material!" The "Otherness" faithfully aided him. "Someone seems to be writing for me most of the time," he wrote, and added, "No one need ever feel sorry for me. I have already been paid over and over" (letters to Frank Luther Mott, September 28, 1920; March 18, 1922; and April 10, 1921). He felt entirely at home with his subject. In 1918 he had met Curly, Custer's scout, and he entered a "blood brother" pact with an exchange of rings. Even earlier he had gone up the Missouri River as a deck hand with the famous Captain Marsh. His research helped him live these events in the writing, and he thought he "got the fighting on paper" (letter to Mott, January 4, 1922).

The Song of the Indian Wars describes dramatically the gradual displacement of Indians as white men moved into the West. It covers the period from 1866, the end of the Civil War, to 1877 and the death of Crazy Horse, the "last great Sioux." As the story moves from episode to episode, shifting focus from red men to white, sympathetically picturing all participants as trying to survive in a struggle that is fully understood by none, it builds the overriding mood of impersonal compassion that informs the great classical epics. The *Song* presents a panorama of swift action, but Neihardt so carefully controls the stance that in the midst of wild battle action the reader suddenly sees in sharp detail a trooper sitting cross-legged like a tailor, calmly picking jammed bullets out of a gun and reloading, or the reader hears "curses muttered lest a stout heart break" (p. 97), when men are dying in the rain at Beecher's Island. In the early sections, Neihardt focuses on Indians in council deciding upon policy. The deliberations are fired with the drama of oratory in the clash between the wise counsel of Spotted Tail, who thinks of women and children who cannot die in battle and who therefore urges concession, and the scornful eloquence of Red Cloud, great Oglala orator, who denounces white man's greed and who issues a thrilling call for war.

Specific battles in the *Song* include an attack on a log train; the Fetterman massacre; the tense Wagon Boxes fight; the Battle of Beecher's Island, where the tide of war turned in the white man's favor; the massacre of Crazy Horse's village; and the Custer battle. Each scene reveals a different facet of war, and in each the sympathy shifts between troopers and Indians. Fetterman boasts with unbecoming arrogance that with eighty men he could "wipe out the whole Sioux nation"; yet when his men clink into ambush and he falls, his writhing death stirs compassion. At the Wagon Boxes men on both sides show themselves to be stouthearted. Outnumbered troopers stoically rig shoelace nooses around a toe to shoot themselves in extremity, since the rifles are too long for suicide by hand. The Sioux, equally brave, charge vainly into the continuous fire of the new Springfield rifles. The victims of war, both red and white, claim sympathy. Moers the surgeon lingers in pain, neglected by Death, who is too busy to attend him. Crazy Horse's people, returning to their gutted village, mourn their dead babies; and practical women scavenge for anything useful against winter cold.

The last sections of the *Song* are devoted to Crazy Horse, Neihardt's favorite Indian hero, whose aura of sacred power awes the Indians. He and his people maintain their freedom until starvation drives them into the Reservation, but his reputation raises hope that he may again lead resistance. He is lured to Fort Robinson by false assurance of safety to talk with the commandant. But actually he is to be imprisoned. When he resists being pushed into a cell, he is bayoneted by a trooper and carried, dying, into a small office. Lying on the floor, he sings his death chant and dies. Then his old parents are admitted to the office and allowed to grieve over him. Neihardt composed the chant from eyewitness accounts, chiefly Major Lemly's, and the poet made his own additions in order to create a lyric reprise of the Indian experience. The actual scene had so touched Lemly that he decided to request a transfer, and Neihardt's description conveys the pathos: sounds and rhythm intensify the emotional tone to almost overpowering grief.

This *Song*, about ordinary men who are transformed into heroes by events and who are struggling against impossible odds to preserve values they cherish, represents the universal striving to sustain life, and the pathos of a world where brave and noble men must attack each other in a mistaken attempt to satisfy the same deep human needs. This *Song* raises the level of spiritual values in the *Cycle* to impersonal sacrifice for the general good —the Virgilian social ideal. Throughout the writing, Neihardt's "Otherness" guided him, and when he finished on April 23, 1924, he wrote at the end of the manuscript, "Thanks!"

Feeling like a ghost in search of a body, Neihardt waited for the "filling up" process to prepare him for the Messiah *Song*. In the interim he wrote two lectures on poetry, published as *Poetic Values: Their Reality and Our Need of Them* (1925), to present at the University of Nebraska in fulfillment of his obligation as Honorary Professor of Poetry. These lectures form a substantial part of his poetics and defend poetry against an apathetic world on the grounds that poetic insight in both poets and readers endows mankind with the values necessary for making wise decisions.

Before he could undertake the next Song, Neihardt faced the pressure to assure his family a steady income, and he turned again to literary editorships as a solution. For several months during the spring of 1926 he edited a page for the Kansas City *Journal-Post,* and in the fall he accepted a permanent position with the St. Louis *Post-Dispatch.* Recognizing the advantage of association with a paper that enjoyed national prestige, he established his family in the suburbs of St. Louis and gave his attention to writing and editing book reviews.

Theoretically, he was empowered to work at home in the mornings on his own writing, but editing the page usurped all his time, and the Messiah *Song* remained unwritten except for the 500 lines he had produced before he left Branson. Whenever the *Cycle* came to a standstill, Neihardt's spirits suffered. Much as he enjoyed the *Post-Dispatch* position, he muttered darkly about "scurvy civilization," and in unguarded moments he railed at the world as a "damned money-trap." The years in St. Louis occasioned some of his most fractious utterances. In 1931 he arranged a leave and protected his seclusion until 1935, part of the time conducting his page by mail. His spirits improved at once. Returning to work on the epic invariably restored his disposition and his faith in humanity.

During his vacation in 1930, Neihardt had visited Pine Ridge Reservation to talk with the Sioux and to enrich his understanding of the Messiah movement. The trip proved momentous, for he met Black Elk, who was the last holy man of the Oglalas and who was, as Neihardt said, the most significant single influence upon his life and thought. Black Elk usually refused interviews, but he greeted Neihardt as an expected friend "sent" to learn about the world of the spirit. Black Elk's teaching profoundly impressed Neihardt, who returned to Pine Ridge the following summer to resume the talks. Black Elk had adopted Neihardt as his "spiritual son," the instrument to preserve the wisdom and culture of the Sioux.

Calling Neihardt a "word sender" whose words fell like rain and made the world greener wherever they touched it, Black Elk disclosed the vision that had governed his life. He paid Neihardt a tribute, for holy men seldom related power visions even to other members of the tribe. Indeed, revealing sacred matters to a white man was all but unthinkable. On the second visit Neihardt and two of his daughters were made members of the Oglala tribe in a sacred ceremony followed by traditional feasting, dancing, and oratory.

24

From his conversations with the holy man came Neihardt's most widely known work, *Black Elk Speaks* (1931). The book presents a charming picture of Indian life in the old days, as well as a moving account of the Indian wars as experienced by the Sioux. The most important section is devoted to the vision. According to Sioux custom, a boy underwent puberty rites at twelve. After a purification ceremony he was isolated on a hill to fast and await a vision, frequently in the form of a dream, to guide his life. Afterward he reported the dream to a holy man for interpretation.

Black Elk's vision departed from the ordinary by occurring when he was nine, without the rites. In the vision as described in the book, he is conducted into the sky to the Six Grandfathers, or Powers, representing the four directions, the Earth, and the Sky. Each Grandfather gives him a sacred object, symbol of a power vested in Black Elk to preserve his people: the power to make or destroy life, the power to cleanse and heal, the power to know peace and understanding, the power to unite and make flourish, and the power to endure. Black Elk travels the black road of worldly difficulties and the red road of spirit, plants a sacred red stick at the center where the roads intersect, and sees it branch into a tree, filled with singing birds, that shelters people and creatures mingling in harmony.

In a remarkable section similar to the apocalyptic visions of the Bible or Blake's prophetic poems, Black Elk sees the tree withered and the people at war. Then, healed by a sacred herb, dancing together, people and creatures rejoice in a day of happiness that Black Elk is to bring about. The horses of four different colors that accompany him throughout the vision perform a dance, and a sacred rain "blesses" the people. Black Elk stands at the center of the earth and sees the hoop of his people as one of many hoops, all sheltered by the flowering tree. He is given a sacred herb that will enable him to undertake and do anything. It is the herb of understanding. When he drops it on the earth it takes root and sends up colored rays that dispel darkness. Reminded of his responsibilities by the Grandfathers, Black Elk is returned to earth. He had been in a twelve-day trance. To Neihardt the most remarkable feature of the vision was that Black Elk saw the hoop of his people as one of many, where people of all colors were united under the flowering tree, for at the time of the vision Black Elk had never seen people of other races.

Frightened by the impossible assignment which the vision imposes upon him, Black Elk conceals his "dream" for some time, since he thinks no one will believe him. Several times as he grows up, he shows unusual powers, frequently by warning of danger; but the troubles of his people preoccupy him, and he pushes aside his special powers. At thirteen he shares the general devotion to Crazy Horse, and he takes part in the Rosebud battle against Crook, the sun dances, and the Custer fight. Fleeing with his people into the hills, he suffers the miseries of the defeated.

At sixteen, when thunder beings remind him of his vision, he confides in the holy man Black Road, who instructs him to perform his vision, repeating the horse dance with horses of four colors coming from the four directions and four maidens carrying sacred symbols of Black Elk's powers into a dancing circle. The ceremony is performed, and Black Elk, relieved of his fears, becomes a healer. The horse dance, which is actually a rite to bring the rain that blessed the people in the vision, becomes a rite that demonstrates Black Elk's powers. He hears the rumors of a Messiah and listens to the reports of men sent to investigate, but he hesitates to accept the story until he sees in the ghost dance at Wounded Knee Creek convincing similarities to his own vision. He joins the Messiah movement that ends in the massacre at Wounded Knee. As Black Elk says, the real disaster was the dying of the people's dream in bloody mud.

In a moving epilog Neihardt describes Black Elk's last visit to the "center of the earth," Harney Peak, where he stood in the vision. On the way Black Elk comments that if any remnant of his power remains, the thunder beings should send a little rain —an unlikely prospect on a blazing day in the depths of drought. Standing on the summit of the peak, the sacred pipe in his hand, Black Elk prays to the Grandfathers, confessing "with running tears" that he has failed to make the tree bloom. He pleads for his people that if even a little root of the tree lives it may bloom and fill with singing birds. Sending a "feeble voice in sorrow," he concludes, "O make my people live!" He has asked for a sign that his powers are not entirely lost, and as he prays gray clouds gather, low thunder sounds, and chilly rain falls.

When it appeared in 1931, *Black Elk Speaks* received glowing reviews from such writers as Constance Lindsay Skinner, Bruce Catton, Stanley Vestal, and Marquis Childs, all of whom saw the vision as a prototype. But Neihardt again was ahead of the times. The book did not gain prominence until Carl Jung's enthusiasm brought it to the attention of psychologists and anthropologists. The upsurge of interest in Indian culture doubtless helped to make it an underground classic, to use Dick Cavett's words. After Neihardt was interviewed on the Cavett show, *Black Elk Speaks* became a best seller. Selections from it now appear in anthologies with increasing frequency.

The religion and mysticism of *Black Elk Speaks* are now attracting scholarly interest aside from their psychological or sociological implications. Robert F. Sayre, in "Vision and Experience in *Black Elk Speaks*" (*College English,* February 1971), analyzes the possible influence of the Sioux culture upon the vision. His conclusion that the vision was essentially poetry and that the Grandfathers were "supreme fictions" (p. 534) would not be Neihardt's, but Sayre rightly describes Neihardt as "one of the most knowledgeable and sensitive students of

American Indian culture the dominant American culture ever produced" (p. 514).

The problem of accrediting the vision arises from its not coming literally true; Black Elk himself believed that he had failed. Neihardt was not so sure. He lived to see his book impress hundreds of readers, and he concluded that if Black Elk was given powers to unite peoples with the sacred herb of understanding, perhaps in telling his story to Neihardt, Black Elk had made his people live.

In another article, *"Black Elk Speaks*: and So Does John Neihardt" (*Western American Literature,* Winter 1972), Sally Mcclusky pleads effectively for studies of *Black Elk Speaks* as literature, not as psychology or anthropology. A study of Neihardt's literary techniques holds surprises, for the deceptively simple style flows across a web of metaphor in rhythms and sound patterns keyed to reinforce the meaning. *Black Elk Speaks* is unique for several reasons, but perhaps primarily for Neihardt's skill in blending the authenticity of a participant with the empathy of an outsider. By using a frame structure, he submerges himself to make the story seem all Black Elk's. At the same time, by returning to the frame, he reminds the reader that the story comes through a listener. Adjustments in the language suggest Indian cadence and idiom that increase the feeling that Black Elk is speaking, but in the rhythm and emotional overtones, Neihardt conveys his own warm sympathy and compassion without suggesting self-pity in the Indians.

As soon as *Black Elk Speaks* was completed, Neihardt went eagerly to work on the Messiah *Song,* the story he thought more lyrical than the other epics, and more beautiful. He had announced the theme to Julius House five years before—the triumph of spirit through apparent defeat—and he described the subject as "the greatest of all human stories, a whole race upon the cross" (letters to House, January 31, 1926 and February 9, 1931). When the talks with Black Elk opened luminous new vistas, he recognized a more profound theme: building on the *Wars, The Messiah* would become not merely an Indian epic but the "whole trajectory of the human spirit through the world" (letter to House, September 11, 1932). He was writing by the middle of January 1932, and in September reported that whatever helped him was aiding him more faithfully than ever. Moreover, the power of the theme satisfied him that the *Song* said what he wanted to say.

The Song of the Messiah begins ten years after the death of Crazy Horse. The despairing Indians see in the return of spring only a "cruel beauty" disguising "empty promise" (p. 3). Starving reservation warriors grip plows with the force of hatred as red men endure purposeless existence. The first section, a "monody of woe," establishes the Indian mood: they see the earth old and dying.

Neihardt wrote the *Song* in the hardest years of the depression, and the descriptions, denuded of color except in memory scenes, rise from his observation of country parched by drought and devastated by dust storms. He had only to look about him to see gaunt corn stalks like mothers "widowed in the silk," or crows feasting beside "dusty water-holes" (p. 4). In the thirties, when many people clutched at impossible hopes in such movements as Father Divine's or the Townsend Plan, Neihardt could understand the Indian susceptibility in the 1880's to rumors that a Messiah rejected by white men was returning to save Indians. When the material world fails, as Neihardt said, the promise of salvation through spritual force gains credibility from the deep human need for some sort of hope.

In the *Song,* miserable Indians are stirred by rumors of a Messiah in the person of the Piute Wovoka, who had "died and yet not died," who had talked with God, and brought back the message of salvation. The Sioux send four men to investigate the rumor. The four men are based upon real people, since Neihardt's research, embellished by what he learned from Black

29

Elk, provided clear information. Neihardt uses the men to represent different points of view: Good Thunder is the genuine mystic; Kicking Bear, the fanatic, more than willing to believe; Yellow Breast, the realist demanding evidence; and Short Bull, the bustling opportunist, eager to lead a movement.

When the four return, their accounts vary according to the temperaments of the men, but all agree that Wovoka seemed an ordinary man until he spoke. Then he seemed transformed, but afterward again became ordinary. Good Thunder saw him burning as if his body were made of light, and Good Thunder reports Wovoka's vision of a paradise strikingly like that of Black Elk's vision, where even grass was holy and where, under a spreading tree, a red man with his tears brought to bloom the holy flower of pain and united in harmony all living things. Kicking Bear, the fanatic, is convinced that Wovoka himself is Jesus returned, for he has seen scars on Wovoka's palms and a spear wound in his side. Yellow Breast, the realist, speaks of the strangeness when Wovoka spoke, and of the look of wonder on faces of believers. Yellow Breast himself is not fully convinced until, in a vision which the entire party experienced together, he sees his dead father and hears him say, "Believe, my son!" Short Bull, the opportunist, tells the story that Neihardt heard from Black Elk of Wovoka's focusing attention on a hat, disclosing in and through its crown a green world of singing rivers, happy valleys, and rejoicing creatures. Short Bull accepts all rumors, claims spirit power of his own, and urges immediate action.

The reports differ, but all suggest that something inexplicable happened. Even the judicious man is convinced. Red Cloud, now old and no longer blazing with defiance, warns that the visions do not promise earthly paradise. But the fever to believe has risen, and the Sioux join the ghost dance intended to unite Indians with their dead relatives, who appear to them in the trance induced by the dancing. The dead are to come to life and assist in driving out white men. This belief is the most pitiable feature of the movement, for the Indians think they will be invincible with the assistance of their dead, who obviously cannot be killed twice. Neihardt establishes the sincerity of the Indians by describing skeptical bystanders drawn into the circle by the unearthly joy of the dancers, and by treating ironically the intrusion of the government agent who orders the dancing stopped. "Can the dead be jailed?" the Indians ask, and continue dancing.

Roused by rumors that Sitting Bull plans resistance, the young men decide to fight. Unfortunately, the false rumors of Sitting Bull's intent are credited by the white men, and the Indian police are ordered to arrest him. Neihardt's description of Sitting Bull's death presents a microcosm of the Indian tragedy: Sitting Bull reviews the old days with his friends, tells the familiar stories, receives portents of danger, and awaits his prophesied doom without fear. He denounces white men as led by their most able tricksters and liars and as blind to their own danger. When they have "stolen all the grass," their "starving people shall become a beast" (p. 79) —prophetic words for Americans concerned about depleted natural resources. When the soldiers arrive, Sitting Bull meets his death courageously. The watching Indians later see his ghostly figure sweep across the sky and disappear behind the distant mountains.

In the last scenes of the *Song*, the starving band led by Sitanka flee toward Wounded Knee, their "sick hope" of an earthly paradise fixed on Kicking Bear's promises. The hope is dashed, for Kicking Bear's starving people have surrendered. Still, as they approach Wounded Knee, Sitanka, feverish with pneumonia, urges belief in the real message of the Spirit and prays for vision to learn from the suffering. Sitanka has found the herb of understanding. Even if the soldiers come to kill, he tells the people, they are brothers, and the Indians must love them. When the band comes upon the soldiers at Wounded Knee,

Sitanka's vision seems to become real. The Soldier Chief dispenses food, wood, and water to all, and he also supplies medicine for the children and the gravely ill Sitanka. In euphoric bliss the exhausted people sink into untroubled sleep, warmed by the soldier's fires. When Sitanka wakes, he sees through his tent flap the miracle come true—an enchanted scene of children unafraid and people moving about in a happy murmur of normal activity.

The sharpest irony of the Wounded Knee tragedy is its needlessness, for the miracle could have been true. The soldiers were willing to be kind: their compassion was stirred, and the peace might have been kept but for the recklessness of a recalcitrant youth. When the Indians are told to stack their guns, Yellow Bird shoots a trooper, and slaughter follows. At the end, however, Sitanka's death turns victory into defeat, for Sitanka has seen the white radiance of the Spirit's meaning. As a soldier clubs him to death with a gun butt, he struggles to say, "My brother!" The soldiers march away and snow covers the bloody field.

Neihardt always thought *The Song of the Messiah* was his best work. It is about more than an incident in Indian-white relations and about more than a delusion of Indian tribes that the Messiah had abandoned their enemies and returned to succor them. The *Song* is about the universal problem of man trying to reach his dreams. Out of his suffering and despair, man mistakenly seeks to direct the valid force of spiritual power toward worldly ends it was never meant to serve.

Neihardt poses the question crucial to all men in an anxious, befuddling world: *what is real?* Through the Messiah story he contrasts the shadowy ordinary world with the lighted world of spirit to say in multiple ways—through the events, the imagery, and the symbolism—that spiritual force is reality, for it brings the understanding that dispels all fear and unites men with nature in a cosmic whole. The theme follows the Christian ethic, but it is so fused with the impact of Black Elk's vision that the theology extends beyond the Christian doctrine. In one of his prefaces Neihardt suggested that the *Song* might be considered a social document, and he believed that his suggestion should be heeded at a time when social theory could profit from an injection of spiritual insight.

In the late summer of 1935, Neihardt returned to St. Louis for another stint at the *Post-Dispatch,* and he temporarily abandoned hope of plunging into the final epic. This newspaper interlude allowed him to enjoy family life without the daemon prodding, and it allowed him to build up financial resources that turned out to be sorely needed. When he left the paper in the summer of 1938 and returned to Branson, he depended again upon lecture tours for a living. By judicious arrangement of schedules, he managed to begin the last epic in September.

Neihardt had made extensive preparation for *The Song of Jed Smith.* When he finished *The Song of Three Friends* in 1918, he had acceded to the request of his publisher to prepare a prose work on mountain men for the school market. The book was to be historically accurate, centered on Jed Smith as hero, and fictionalized only where fiction could enrich without distorting facts. The resulting book, *The Splendid Wayfaring* (1920), was well received as an "American Odyssey," and the research provided the materials for the *Song.* In the summer of 1937, Neihardt traveled with Mona and daughters Hilda and Alice through the Jed Smith country to examine South Pass, the Salt Desert, and as much of Smith's route as possible in the time available.

Neihardt had thought the *Song* out in detail at least a year before he began to write, for in 1937 he sketched out the format to a friend. He had decided on the frame structure he frequently used in short stories. Some years after Smith's death, three old trappers, Jed's former companions, meet at the site of the 1825 Rendezvous, sit around a campfire sharing a jug of Oh-be-joyful or "Taos lightning," and talk about old times. Jed's story emerges through their reminiscences as they grow drunk. The three men represent different levels of perception, and through the educated man the "finer things" of the poem emerge. When the other two have thrown "sidelights of cruder vision" on Jed, the educated man "says a mouthful about human life and destiny" (letter to Judge Vinsonhaler, Omaha *World-Herald,* September 19, 1937). No one hears him, for the other two are snoring.

In 1939 Neihardt began to write the *Song.* In *The Messiah* he had continued his established meter because, as part of the *Wars,* it should preserve unity. He considered shifting to unrhymed verse in *Jed,* possibly with interpolated lyric passages, but after deliberation he decided to keep the *Cycle* style and follow his intent to build the background as by "conversational accident" (letter to Enid and Ollie Fink, December 9, 1938). Letting the reader overhear "three guys gassing and getting tighter" enabled him to use a light touch that was more effective than a serious tone would have been to let poetry "break through" the common words (letter to Enid and Ollie Fink, January 5, 1939). The happy result is an easy conversational flow where the mood shifts freely from hearty banter to intense seriousness, and the talking poetry pulls the reader into the scene. Men and animals come alive in the trapper idiom and in the sharp details of setting.

As Neihardt's almost daily account of the writing shows, the "Otherness" attended him well. He frequently had the sensation of recording something already written as if he were receiving it by dictation. He seemed to be traveling with the party, seeing the country as they saw it. His letters used participant verbs, as when he wrote, "We've entered the great central desert after crossing the High Sierras, and it's getting to be pretty damned hot" (letter to Enid and Ollie Fink, June 25,

1940). During the delays occasioned by lecture tours, Neihardt relieved his impatience by turning to his hobby of polishing and setting gems. He thought that the lapidary work aided his writing. The last part of the *Song* dragged out, with the strain of Neihardt's financial problems and frustrations severe enough to draw a rare comment from Mona: "No one can guess what a long hard pull that Cycle has been!" (letter to Alice Neihardt from Mona, January 6, 1940). It was finished in the spring of 1941, and Neihardt realized with something like shock that his life work was ended.

The Song of Jed Smith covers the adventures of Jed, not chronologically, but through reminiscences of his three old friends that gradually build a picture of Jed. Two of the three, Bob Evans and Art Black, are real people; the third, Squire, is Neihardt's creation. Each represents a different level of sensitivity and understanding. Squire, youngest and lowest on the scale, concentrates on food, drink, and excitement; Art Black, the eldest, makes practical judgments and leaves philosophy to dreamers; Bob Evans, the educated man searching for meaning in life, hovers between faith and doubt. All three bear the heroic stamp, for they cope resourcefully with the rigorous demands of their chosen life. The fur trade was no vocation for weaklings.

Their reminiscences largely concern the journeys of 1826 and 1827, but they begin with recollections of trappers and descriptions of Jed—his hawk nose, clean-shaven face, and "lean six-feet of man-stuff" (p. 11). A dreamer as well as a competent leader, he saw the West as a blank page for the writing of new history. His old friends judge him "man a-plenty" despite his propensity for reading the Bible and disappearing into the woods for private prayer. At various times Neihardt returns to the frame to allow the men to exchange raillery or discuss philosophy, according to their lights. Recalling the crossing of South Pass, Squire introduces the theme of the *Song*. He describes the feeling emanating from Jed that affects all the men—a sense of awe and mystery in the universe. Black calls it something "thrilling" that people know before they learn "so much that isn't so," and Evans sums it up as the "humble wisdom that is wonder" (pp. 18 and 19).

The events of the story serve chiefly to illuminate the character of Jed, but they are also interesting in themselves. As with his portrayal of the awe of the men at crossing South Pass (1824), Neihardt colors history in some scenes, for actually, as Wallace Stegner noted (*Mormon Country,* p. 241), the explorers only later realized that they had crossed the pass. But Neihardt followed truth of a different order, for the crossing *was* momentous, whether the trappers realized it or not.

Squire also describes Jed's encounter with a bear and the discovery of Salt Lake, where the men dispute whether or not it is the Pacific. Black's memories include their crossing the desert to the sea in 1826, enduring agonies of thirst and hunger, watching the horses collapse and die, and stumbling through burning heat in a timeless delirium, dreaming of wells and running streams. They note Jed's refreshed look after prayer, but they themselves most rejoice when they come upon pools or streams. They do listen to Jed's impromptu religious services, where he makes the Bible's words seem to come alive.

Black tells of friendly Indians reviving the men with food and water, then giggling with delight over trade wares like mirrors and shiny knives. Black almost envies the contentment of a Piute who feeds them from his garden, and he contrasts the welcome they receive at a Mohave village in 1826 with the ruthless murder of ten men by the Mohaves the next year. He recalls Silas Gobel, the blacksmith, drowning in a flood of warriors, wielding his club until they close over him. Jed and eight others, already out on the river, escape.

Evans, who knew Jed best, recounts the trek which he and Gobel made with Jed across the desert to the 1827 Rendezvous, leaving the main party in California. He describes the grim struggle across the icy Sierras, urged on by Jed's confident encouragement. Beyond the mountains their journey becomes a tortured search for water, relieved now and then by the discovery of a brook. Evans recalls the mules, too tired to eat, leaning against each other, dead asleep standing up.

He describes also a significant moment on a ridge when he and Jed, almost at the end of endurance, search for a spring. They miss the spring, and Evans sees Jed momentarily desperate, but in a flash of insight Evans realizes that Jed's "breaking manhood" is stronger than his "unbroken might." Then he realizes the depth of his feeling for Jed. Evans has learned that human imperfection is essential to true strength—and to love. The three struggle on, inspired by Jed's faith. Dizzy with heat and thirst, their tongues too swollen to let them swallow the last of the dried meat, they lose track of time and seem too float in a troubled dream of lakes and wells. When Evans collapses, Jed and Silas go on to seek a spring, and Jed returns with water to rescue Evans. The men at last reach the Rendezvous, haggard and gaunt.

Black takes up the story of the 1827 events. Jed returns to the men waiting at San Gabriel and the party moves up the Pacific coast into Oregon. At the Umpqua River, however, all of them, except for Jed and Black, who have gone ahead to scout for a trail, are massacred by the Umpquas.

Well along toward drunken stupor, Squire and Black recall sleepily that Jed had intended to retire, but that he made one last trip in 1831 to finance his brothers in a venture and met his death on the Cimarron River. Evans, the only one awake, tells the story of Jed's death. He had heard of it the next year and had set out to follow the sketchy details picked up from Indians in Santa Fe.

For reasons consistent with the influence of psychic experience upon Neihardt's creative processes, his description of Jed's last moments departs from the account as given by historian Dale Morgan (*Jedediah Smith and the Opening of the West*, 1953). Neihardt knew F. W. H. Myers' exhaustive treatment of psychic research (*Human Personality and Its Survival of Bodily Death*, 1903), and had studied various sources dealing with psychic phenomena. He frequently visited mediums, and without being credulous he accepted the validity of psychic experience. While he was writing *Jed Smith*, a medium surprised him by saying, "That fellow you're writing about didn't die the way you think." When he urged her to explain, she gave him the version he decided to use in the *Song*: Jed had left the party to seek water in the dry bed of the Cimarron, and when he knelt to dig, a band of Comanches fell upon him and left him in a huddle of blood and feathers, with just enough strength to crawl to the shade of a sandstone ledge topped by a huge rock. The Indians, returning to collect Jed's horse and gun, rolled the boulder down upon him. On his trip in 1937 Neihardt found a spot that fitted this description. The *Song* closes with the two "louts" snoring by the dying fire and the wail of Evans' little dog, mourning with his master.

The Song of Jed Smith concerns more than the adventures of a hero, however authentic. As he began it, Neihardt believed that he could say all he had ever wanted to say. He envisioned a "glorified character sketch" with overtones of meaning connected with "Otherness" (letter to Enid and Ollie Fink, December 9, 1938). The significance of the *Song* lies in what Evans says about human life and destiny. In the Messiah *Song*, Neihardt had developed his theme of spiritual understanding as key to the universe, and *Jed Smith* extends the theme to encompass the effect of spiritual forces in the individual life, where ultimately it must function.

As Neihardt's "cosmic man," Jed unites the two worlds of "Otherness" and practical daily affairs, and the real point is his effect upon his fellow trappers. Even the imperceptive Squire senses through Jed that the universe holds more for men than physical pleasures. Black reinforces the theme by his hardheaded respect for Jed's reverence and ability to bring alive a truth that is real "because it isn't" (p. 8). Evans is the key character, for the thoughtful man, hovering between faith and doubt, provides the real test of faith. Evans is almost persuaded. Once he dreams of a yucca tree in a rain of "living glory" and comprehends how it can make beauty from pain, and another time he sees a rattlesnake with "fangs of fear" and realizes that it is guarding its own good against a world "neither understood nor understanding" (pp. 92 and 94). All three men learn from Jed that goals are less important than the journeying.

Jed Smith is the ideal hero for Neihardt's purpose, since he stood out among the mountain men in both competence and integrity in a brutal world. Jed's ability to corral rowdy trappers to listen meekly while he reads the Bible testifies to his strength of character. His humanism appears in his disapproval of scurvy talk and in his insistence upon treating Indians "the same as folks" (p. 37). Through Jed's effect on others, Neihardt pursues his theme that man is secure in the cosmos, linked to every atom of a universe of wonder.

Neihardt's treatment of mountain men in the *Cycle* parallels in many respects the picture drawn by such writers as Frederick Manfred, A. B. Guthrie, Jr., and Vardis Fisher. They seem to have read the same sources—Beckwourth, Ruxton, Sage, Chittenden, Eastman, Larpenteur, and possibly the Harrison Rogers journals. Neihardt's trappers are stirred by the same lure of adventure, delight in wilderness freedom, and deep love of the country itself. He devotes less attention to details of raw brutality, though he does not discount violence. Hugh Glass clubbing off wolves and various battle scenes are brutal enough, but Neihardt depends more frequently upon suggestion than upon graphic detail. He elevates the character of some trappers—Mike Fink, for example—but not to the point of destroying credibility. Neihardt's warm, compassionate tone most closely resembles Manfred's. His portrayals of mountain men differ from those of other writers chiefly because the novel form makes different demands from those of the epic. Novels require fully rounded heroes, but in epics the character is individualized only enough to be believable. A hero must be universalized to represent human experience and the heroic potential of all men.

In the years after the last *Song,* Neihardt faced the most difficult period of his life. He was sixty; his funds were exhausted, and he had no job. The war put an end to lecture possibilities, and illness added to Neihardt's discouragement. But as his health improved, his stubborn pioneer spirit revived. Moved by an outraged determination to prove once more that he could survive against odds, he went to Chicago in the fall of 1942 in search of any job he could find.

For a time he read manuscripts for *Esquire,* until weakened vision made the work impossible. He tried several incongruous positions, including a desk job at the Iron Fireman Stoker Company and a summer of camp counseling for the YMCA. At the camp he produced a pageant based upon Black Elk's vision. It was so successful that in the fall he was appointed to manage two YMCA outposts in the roughest section of Chicago. His effectiveness with young toughs proved spectacular. The boys called him "Mr. John" and accepted his guidance with affection.

He grew fond of his "ornery cusses," but in November 1943, he went to consult John Collier, director of the Office of Indian Affairs, which was located in Chicago for the duration of the war. Collier wasted no time in appointing Neihardt Director of Information for the Office. Neihardt went to work in February, and his financial stresses were ended. He remained with the Service for several years, editing the publication *Indians at Work,* writing official reports, and gathering materials for an Indian history. His visits to reservations enabled him to help with solutions to many problems and to collect materials for later writing.

When the Indian Office was returned to Washington at the close of the war, Neihardt went home to Branson, relieved to escape the noise and bustle of Chicago. In 1947 he moved to a beautiful farm near Columbia, Missouri, where he could enjoy the company of old friends, notably Frank Luther Mott, then Dean of the School of Journalism at the University of Missouri. Neihardt named his farm Skyrim, built a Sioux prayer garden in front of the house, and added barns to accommodate horses. In 1948, when he joined the faculty of the University as Poet in Residence and Lecturer in English, he began a new career as a teacher. His classes on Epic America, poetry writing, and the critical essay proved popular, and to his surprise, he became a television regular in a series on poetry. Strangers greeted him on the street, and he was repeatedly asked to televise programs in Lincoln, Nebraska.

In Columbia, Neihardt finished the novel he had begun in Branson, *When the Tree Flowered* (1951). Based upon materials the author had gathered from Old Eagle Elk and his friends at Pine Ridge Reservation, the novel presents a picture of Sioux life and culture through memories of the main character, Eagle Voice. He describes charming scenes of Indian life—buffalo hunts, evenings of feasting and story-telling, and the daily work of women preparing hides for clothing or cutting strips of meat for winter. Through the story runs the romance of Eagle Voice and his playmate Tashima, begun when they were children, interrupted when the tribes separated, and resumed at the end of the story, after the Battle of Wounded Knee.

Neihardt relieves the darkening mood of the story by interpolating legends and folklore, sometimes humorous, sometimes mystic, sometimes illustrative of laws and customs. For example, he explains the Sioux governing system as grounded in religion. Since the hoop of the people was sacred, violating the law broke the hoop. Laws were made by a council chosen on merit; only a man of undisputed courage, generosity, and integrity might be made a councilor. The sacred pipe, symbol of honor and truth, carried more force than legal oaths. Vows made in it were absolutely binding, for if the pipe spoke with a forked tongue, who could be trusted? The stories "Falling Star, the Savior" and "Why the Island Was Sacred" blend various myths and legends, including the cause of seasonal changes, the mystique of rain, and the assignment to Indians of Pa Sapa, the Promised Land. The stories bear strong resemblance to fairy tales, myths, and legends common to many cultures.

Neihardt's portrayal of Indians and of Indian life made a significant contribution to literature. His admiration of Sioux culture and his respect for the mysticism of their religion helped to counter stereotypes that had grown up about Indians as noble savages or as treacherous marauders. The rapport which Neihardt had established with the Sioux was accorded to few white men, but the Sioux were willing to talk freely with Neihardt and to let him see the world through their eyes. As various letters in his files show, they considered his picture of them accurate. He felt the keen interest and sympathy observable in the writings of Frank Waters about the Hopi, though Neihardt did not, like Waters, sustain the outsider stance. In passages where Waters adopts the Indian voice, the rhythm and style become much like Neihardt's.

The appearance of the epics in a single volume in 1949 gratified Neihardt's most ardent wish. The individual *Songs* had been favorably reviewed as they appeared, and the publication of the *Cycle* drew widespread praise. Neihardt was criticized for his style in some reviews that noted archaic contractions and inversions, grandiose words, outmoded metrical form, and the inappropriate blending of classical and colloquial language. Other reviewers praised the *Cycle's* richness of expression, authentic idiom, and skillful verse that entirely avoided monotony. The

Songs were labeled epics, and Neihardt was frequently called an American Homer, perhaps most notably in William Rose Benét's pronouncement in the *Saturday Review of Literature:* "Verily the old West has its Homer at last!" (August 13, 1927).

The sharpest objection to Neihardt's style and intent seemed to come from Regionalist critics, but to judge an epic by regionalist standards argues a narrow definition of epic. Clumsy wordings that occur, chiefly in the early epics, are to be regretted, but Neihardt was not falling back upon outdated meter from want of poetic enterprise; he was adapting traditional form to the specific needs of a modern epic. His blending of styles troubled Kenneth Rothwell ("In Search of a Western Epic: Neihardt, Sandburg, and Jaffe as Regionalists and 'Astoriadists'" *(Kansas Quarterly,* Spring 1970), but that blending serves to unite the universality of epic and the idiom and cadence of a modern style.

Neihardt had no retirement years. Mona's death in 1958 saddened him, but his days were soon again filled with activities. He retired from teaching, but he continued to lecture and to appear on television programs. At eighty-one he received a Fulbright award for study in India (an accident prevented him from making the trip), and at ninety he read his poetry to a junior high school audience, and the performance was moving enough to receive six standing ovations. He saw an annual Neihardt Day inaugurated in Bancroft, where his old "office" was converted to a small museum and a prayer garden was planted in the adjoining grounds. He saw two of Mona's busts of him, cast in bronze, placed in the Nebraska Capitol and in the new Fine Arts building at his college in Wayne. His books began to reappear in print, and *Black Elk Speaks,* recognized as a classic, went into translation in twelve languages. His appearance on national television enlarged his audience of admirers. In his late eighties he wrote *All Is But a Beginning* (1972), which is an autobiography about his early memories and the evolution of his philosophy.

At ninety-one Neihardt admitted that his eyes were tired and added that they should be tired; they had seen so many beautiful and wonderful things. He was still making television tapes and speaking to young people, who arrived in busloads to sit on the floor around his wheelchair and to listen to poetry as it was meant to be heard. At his death in 1973, Sioux Indians came, at their own request, to hold a sacred ceremony at the close of the funeral. They performed rites seldom if ever before given for a white man.

Any assessment of Neihardt's permanent contribution to literature entails the obvious hazards of prediction. Reviewers at various times described his work as assured of a permanent place in American literature. Several suggested that he might emerge as the great poet of our time. Historian Dale Morgan credited him with bringing Jed Smith to the attention of the public, and John Myers Myers noted that Neihardt's research had unearthed the letter from Hugh Glass that Manfred quoted in *Lord Grizzly*. But from major literary critics Neihardt received no attention, possibly because he wrote epics in a time of intense critical disapproval of narrative poetry, long poems of any kind, and traditional poetic forms. He ran counter to literary fashion. Moreover, he preferred to isolate himself from literary centers; consequently, he had none of the close connections with critics and other writers that foster critical attention. Still, he held an audience responding directly to him and to his poetry.

Neihardt himself cared most acutely about the future of the *Cycle*. He was not responding to Frank Norris's plea for a frontier epic, as Edgeley W. Todd suggested ("The Frontier Epic: Frank Norris and John G. Neihardt," *Western Humanities Review,* Winter 1959). He had conceived the *Cycle* not as a frontier or Western epic alone, but as an American epic, incorporating heroism with progress toward the spiritual understanding

44

essential to the fulfillment of American ideals. To this end he presented Indians as full participants in the epic struggle, ancestors of modern Americans with as noble a contribution to American ideals as any trapper or white trooper.

The remarkable feature of Neihardt's work is that without the assistance of continuous critical discussion or publishers' advertising, even when his books were out of print, it held an audience. Neihardt lived long enough to see the resurgence of interest in his writings; he was aware of the dissertations and scholarly articles written about him, and he was pleased with the increased sales of his books. If he had been asked to explain that renewed interest, he might have restated the message of all his work: the glory of the race does not depend upon a chosen few born to nobility, but upon the heroic potential in common men and women. This is a view which Neihardt, with some pride, believed to be thoroughly in keeping with the ideals and the traditions of America and of the American West.

Selected Bibliography

Quotations from *A Cycle of the West* are taken from the 1961 printing by The Macmillan Company; all quotations from Neihardt's work are included by arrangement with the Neihardt Trust.

BOOKS BY NEIHARDT: SELECTED

All Is But a Beginning. New York: Harcourt, Brace, Jovanovich, 1972.

Black Elk Speaks. New York: William Morrow & Company, 1932; Lincoln: University of Nebraska Press, 1961; New York: Simon and Schuster, 1972.

A Bundle of Myrrh. New York: The Outing Publishing Company, 1907.

Collected Poems. New York: The Macmillan Company, 1926.

A Cycle of the West. New York: The Macmillan Company, 1949.

The Dawn-Builder. New York: Mitchell Kennerley, 1911.

The Divine Enchantment. New York: James T. White & Co., 1900.

Indian Tales and Others. New York: The Macmillan Company, 1926.

Life's Lure. New York: Mitchell Kennerley, 1914.

The Lonesome Trail. New York: John Lane Company, 1907.

Lyric and Dramatic Poems. Lincoln: University of Nebraska Press, 1965.

Man-Song. New York: Mitchell Kennerley, 1909.

Poetic Values: Their Reality and Our Need of Them. New York: The Macmillan Company, 1925.

The Quest. New York: The Macmillan Company, 1928.

The River and I. New York: G. P. Putnam's Sons, 1910; New York: The Macmillan Company, 1927; Lincoln: University of Nebraska Press, 1968.

The Song of Hugh Glass. New York: The Macmillan Company, 1915.

The Song of the Indian Wars. New York: The Macmillan Company, 1925.

The Song of Jed Smith. New York: The Macmillan Company, 1941.

The Song of the Messiah. New York: The Macmillan Company, 1935.

The Song of Three Friends. New York: The Macmillan Company, 1919.

The Splendid Wayfaring. New York: The Macmillan Company, 1920.

The Stranger at the Gate. New York: Mitchell Kennerley, 1912.

Two Mothers.   New York: The Macmillan Company, 1921.
When the Tree Flowered.   New York: The Macmillan Company, 1952.

SECONDARY SOURCES

The sources for this account of Neihardt's life and work are too extensive to list. Materials include interviews over a period of years, family documents and letters, manuscripts, letters, documents, and clippings in the Neihardt Collection at the Ellis Library, University of Missouri, and in collections in the Nebraska State Historical Society Library, Lincoln. Private collections have been valuable also, notably the Julius T. House Collection owned by Mrs. Mary House Ryskind.

Neihardt's books were widely reviewed in the press, and feature articles frequently appeared in Missouri and Nebraska papers. Critical articles were less frequent, and the only biography in print is Julius T. House's *John G. Neihardt: Man and Poet,* published in Wayne, Nebraska, in 1921. I have written a critical biography that is in press, announced for publication in 1976 (Rodopi Press, Amsterdam). Fred L. Lee's biographical sketch, *John G. Neihardt: The Man and His Western Writings,* privately printed, includes a calendar of significant events and a list of Neihardt's recordings. Current critical articles include the following:

Aly, Lucile F. "John G. Neihardt and Rhetorical Poetry," in *Rhetoric of the People* (Rodopi N.V., 1974) , pp. 139-335.

Black, W. E. "Ethic and Metaphysic: A Study of John G. Neihardt." *Western American Literature,* 2 (Fall 1967) , 205-12.

Flanagan, John T. "John G. Neihardt: Chronicler of the West." *Arizona Quarterly,* 21 (Spring 1965) , 7-20.

Kendrick, M. Slade. "A Poet Looks at the Moon." *The Cornell Plantations,* 20 (Spring 1964) , 9-11.

McClusky, Sally. "Black Elk Speaks: and So Does John Neihardt." *Western American Literature,* 6 (Spring 1972) , 231-42.

Mott, Frank Luther. "Resurgence of Neihardt." *The Quarterly Journal of Speech,* 48 (April 1962) , 198-201.

Rothwell, Kenneth. "In Search of a Western Epic: Neihardt, Sandburg, and Jaffe as Regionalists and 'Astoriadists'." *Kansas Quarterly* 2 (1970) , 53-63.

Todd, Edgeley. "The Frontier Epic: Frank Norris and John G. Neihardt." *Western Humanities Review,* 13 (Winter 1959) , 40-45.